Learn About

ANIMAL HOMES

REEFS

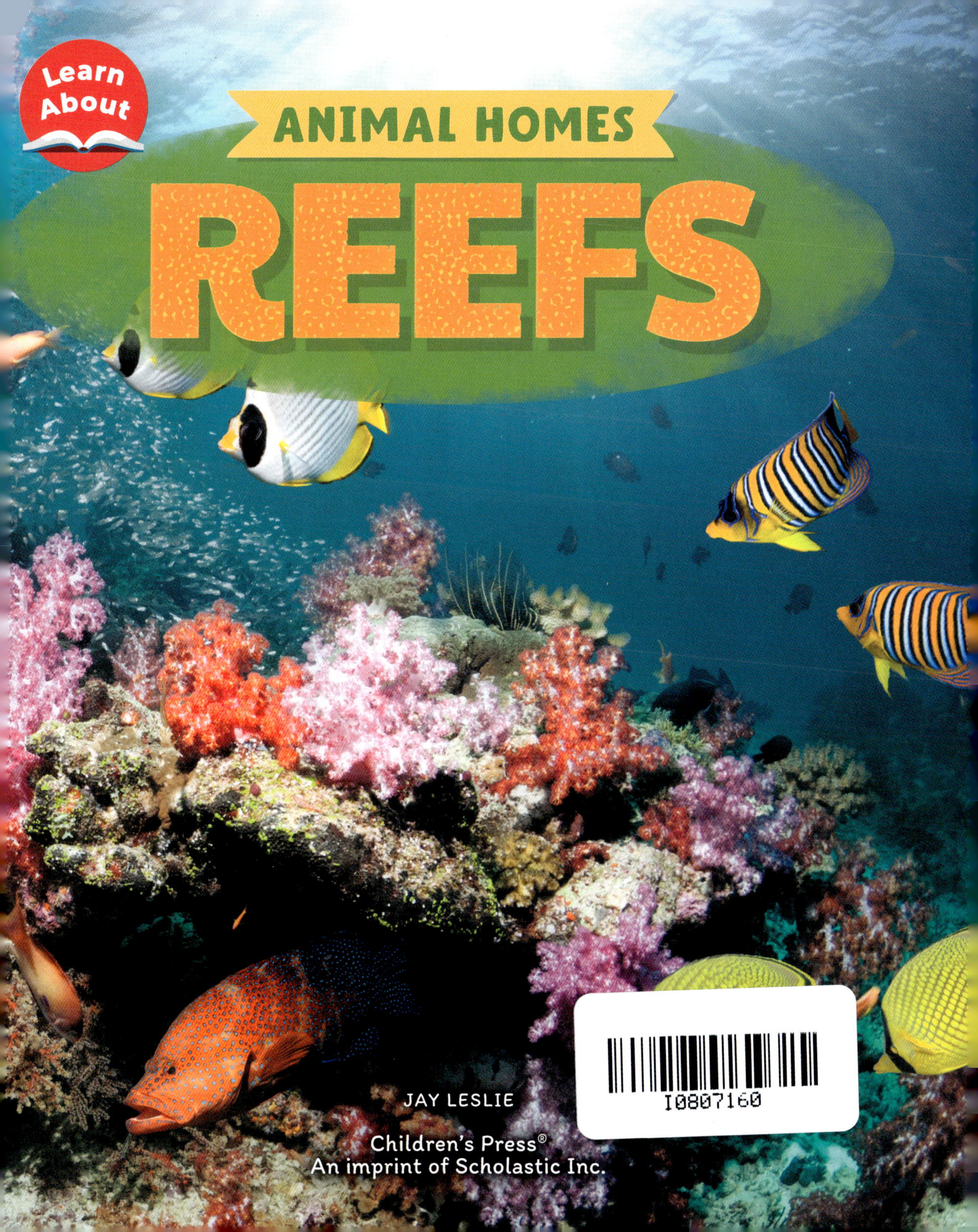

JAY LESLIE

Children's Press®
An imprint of Scholastic Inc.

A special thank-you to the Cincinnati Zoo & Botanical Garden
for their expert consultation.

Library of Congress Cataloging-in-Publication Data available

ISBN 978-1-5461-7742-5 (library binding) | ISBN 978-1-5461-7743-2 (paperback)

10 9 8 7 6 5 4 3 2 1 26 27 28 29 30

Printed in China 62

First edition, 2026

Book design by Kay Petronio

Photos ©: cover, 1: Georgette Douwma/Getty Images; 2: Federico Cabello/Getty Images; 4–5: Georgette Douwma/Getty Images; 7 main: Stephen Frink/Getty Images; 7 inset: Androz Zen/500px/Getty Images; 8–9: Tony Wu/Nature Picture Library/Alamy Images; 9 inset: Androz Zen/500px/Getty Images; 10 top: Mark Chivers/Getty Images; 10 bottom: M Swiet Productions/Getty Images; 11 main: Ralph Pace/Minden Pictures; 11 inset: Reinhard Dirscherl/Getty Images; 12–13: Jeff Rotman/Blue Planet Archive; 13 inset: Reinhard Dirscherl/Getty Images; 14 bottom: Reinhard Dirscherl/ullstein bild/Getty Images; 15 main: Andrey Nekrasov/ZUMA Press Wire/Shutterstock; 15 inset: David Fleetham/VW PICS/Universal Images Group/Getty Images; 16–17: Antonio Busiello/Getty Images; 17 inset: David Fleetham/VW PICS/Universal Images Group/Getty Images; 18 top: Santiago Urquijo/Getty Images; 19 main: Scott Leslie/Minden Pictures; 22: Federico Cabello/Getty Images; 23 main: Alex Mustard/NPL/Minden Pictures; 23 inset: Aleksei Permiakov/Getty Images; 24–25: Norbert Probst/imageBROKER/Getty Images; 25 inset: Aleksei Permiakov/Getty Images; 26: ifish/Getty Images; 27: Douglas Klug/Getty Images; 28: robertcicchetti/Getty Images; 29: Reinhard Dirscherl/Getty Images.

CONTENTS

INTRODUCTION

WELCOME TO THE REEF!

Coral reefs are busy worlds under the sea! Millions of animals live in coral reefs. Most reefs are made from pieces of coral that harden into rock. They are a perfect place for animals to find food and shelter. Reefs also keep them safe from predators. Some animals even help reefs grow. Read on to learn about some of these amazing creatures. Let's dive into this underwater world!

A green sea turtle swims over a colorful coral reef.

Chapter 1

SEAHORSES

FACT FILE

ANIMAL GROUP: Fish

DIET: Carnivore

HABITATS: Coastal waters, reefs, seagrass

FACT!

Seahorses can move their eyes in different directions at the same time.

Pygmy seahorses have bumpy skin. The bumps look just like the coral. Can you see them?

Coral reefs help seahorses stay safe. Seahorses use their tails like little hands. They grab onto the branches of coral. Then they don't float away in the strong ocean waves. Seahorses also use the reef to camouflage. They can change their colors to match the coral. Their skin can be bright orange or purple. This makes them almost invisible to predators.

Seahorses eat all day long. They don't have stomachs to store food. They use their long snouts to suck up tiny shrimp and plankton. Both live in the reef. One seahorse can eat up to 3,000 tiny shrimp in a day!

FACT!

Seahorses are dancers! Male and female seahorses dance together every morning. They can link their tails together.

Male seahorses can have up to 2,000 babies at a time.

Seahorses are special animals. The males have babies. Male seahorses carry eggs in a pouch on their belly. When the eggs are ready, the dad gives birth. The reef protects the babies as they grow up.

Chapter 2

SEA TURTLES

FACT FILE

ANIMAL GROUP: Reptile

DIET: Omnivore

HABITATS: Oceans, reefs, seagrass

FACT!

Sea turtles also eat jellyfish. More than 100 types of jellyfish live in coral reefs.

Hawksbill turtles eat both plants and animals.

Sea turtles are like gardeners for coral reefs. They help coral reefs stay healthy. Green sea turtles eat seagrass. This keeps the grass short and tidy. If seagrass grows too much, it can block the sunlight. Coral reefs need sunlight to grow. Hawksbill turtles eat sponges that live on the reef. This helps coral have enough space to grow. It keeps the reef balanced.

Sea turtles go to the bathroom as they swim. Their waste adds nutrients to the water. These help the coral grow. Sea turtles also spread coral seeds. They eat coral and swim to new areas. Tiny coral pieces are released in their waste. New coral reefs can grow in different places.

FACT!

To lay eggs, a female sea turtle returns to the beach where she hatched. Then she goes back to the reef. The eggs hatch on their own.

Coral reefs keep sea turtles safe. They use reefs to rest and hide from predators. Young turtles often live in reefs, too. The habitat protects them.

Sea turtle babies are called hatchlings.

Chapter 3

MORAY EELS

FACT FILE

ANIMAL GROUP: Fish

DIET: Carnivore

HABITAT: Reefs

FACT!

There are 200 different types of moray eels that live in coral reefs.

The skin color of this moray eel blends into the reef.

Coral reefs are perfect homes for moray eels. These animals have bodies like long ribbons. They can hide in narrow cracks in the reef. These cracks help them escape predators like sharks. Moray eels can be different patterns and colors. They can have spots or stripes. These patterns help them blend into the reef. They use camouflage to stay hidden from predators and prey.

The reef is a perfect hunting ground for moray eels. It is full of small fish and crabs to eat. Moray eels have two sets of jaws. They have one in their mouths and one in their throat. The jaw in their throat grabs prey and pulls it in.

This grouper (left) keeps an eye out for prey. The green moray eel might catch it first!

FACT!

Most moray eels are nocturnal hunters. They come out at night when their prey is less alert.

Moray eels don't just hunt alone. They team up with other fish! They work with groupers to chase prey. Groupers are a type of fish. The moray eel chases prey through tight spaces. The grouper watches the escape routes. Whoever catches the prey eats it!

Chapter 4

LOBSTERS

FACT FILE

ANIMAL GROUP: Invertebrate

DIET: Omnivore

HABITATS: Coastal waters, fresh water, reefs

FACT!

Lobsters shed their shells as they grow!

American lobsters have two large claws. One is stronger. The other is sharper.

During the day, lobsters hide in the coral reef. They squeeze into cracks or under rocks. They stay away from predators, like eels and octopuses. Lobsters have hard shells for protection. They also have long, spiky antennae. Some lobsters have big claws. They use their claws to grab food and defend themselves. Other lobsters, like spiny lobsters, don't have claws. Instead, they use their sharp antennae and fast movements to stay safe.

At night, lobsters come out to explore the reef and look for food. They like to eat crabs, clams, and snails. Lobsters also eat bits of plants and algae. Eating algae helps the reef. If too much algae grows, it can block the sunlight. The coral reef needs sunlight to grow.

FACT!

A lobster may live for close to 100 years.

Lobsters help make homes for other reef creatures, too. They dig burrows in the coral. This creates places for small fish and shrimp to also hide.

A blue lobster crawls out of its hiding place.

Chapter 5

SPONGES

FACT FILE

ANIMAL GROUP: Invertebrate

DIET: Bacteria and plankton

HABITATS: Fresh water, reefs, rocky surfaces

FACT!

Sponges don't move like other animals. Instead, they stay in one spot. The water flows through their bodies.

Can you spot the crab on this bright yellow sponge?

Sponges are natural water filters. These animals clean the water by taking out bacteria. This helps the reef stay healthy. It also gives sea creatures clean water to live in. Sponges turn this bacteria into food. Animals, such as crabs and worms, eat the food. This is called the "sponge loop." Sponges are a big reason why coral reefs are so healthy.

Did you know that sponges also help build reefs? They bind coral and rocks together. This makes the reef stronger. Their bodies act like glue. Sponges are also homes for many reef animals, such as shrimp and small fish. These creatures hide in the sponges' holes and stay safe from predators.

Pufferfish like this one hide inside the holes of sponges.

FACT!

Sponges can filter thousands of gallons of water every day. That is about how much water is in a small backyard swimming pool.

Sponges can be all kinds of shapes and sizes. Some look like barrels. Others look like tubes. And some even look like big fans. Their shapes help them fit into different parts of the reef.

MORE WATER HOMES

CAVES

Sea caves are made by waves hitting weak spots in cliffs. Waves carrying sand and rocks smash against the cliff. This happens again and again. Over time, the water breaks down the rock. This makes the cave bigger and deeper. Animals like reef sharks and stonefish live in the water there.

KELP FORESTS

These underwater forests are made of giant algae. They grow in cool, shallow waters. Kelp can grow up to 18 inches (46 cm) in a single day! That's as long as a children's tennis racket. Kelp forests provide food and shelter for many animals. These include fish, seals, sea otters, and birds.

LODGES

Beaver lodges are like cozy houses in the water. Beavers build them with branches, mud, and leaves. They create dome-shaped homes. These homes look like big piles of sticks on the outside. The entrances are hidden underwater. Beavers can safely swim in and out and away from predators.

ARTIFICIAL REEFS (SHIPWRECKS)

Artificial reefs are made from sunken ships. When a ship sinks, small fish like sardines arrive first. They will make a home inside. Over time, coral, algae, and sponges grow on the ship. This turns it into a busy reef. Soon, bigger fish like sharks come to hunt. Eels and crabs can hide in dark spaces.

REEF CREATURES

Coral reefs are amazing underwater worlds! You've learned about some animals that live in reefs. Seahorses blend in and hang on to the coral. Turtles keep the seagrass tidy. Eels hunt in teams. Lobsters eat algae. Sponges clean the water. These creatures all help the reef stay healthy. You can discover even more reef animals. Visit your local library or an aquarium!

GLOSSARY

antenna (an-TEN-uh) a feeler on the head of an insect

bacteria (bak-TEER-ee-uh) microscopic, single-celled living things that exist everywhere and that can either be useful or harmful

burrow (BUR-oh) a tunnel or hole in the ground made or used as a home by an animal

camouflage (KAM-uh-flahzh) to disguise something so that it blends in with its surroundings

carnivore (KAHR-nuh-vor) an animal that eats meat

coral reef (KOR-uhl reef) a reef made of coral and other materials that have solidified into rock

filter (FIL-tur) a device that cleans liquids or gases as they pass through it

habitat (HAB-i-tat) the place where an animal or a plant is usually found

invertebrate (in-VUR-tuh-brit) an animal without a backbone

nocturnal (nahk-TUR-nuhl) active at night

nutrient (NOO-tree-uhnt) a substance such as a protein, mineral, or vitamin that is needed by people, animals, and plants to stay strong and healthy

omnivore (AHM-nuh-vor) an animal that eats both plants and meat

plankton (PLANGK-tuhn) tiny animals and plants that drift or float in oceans and lakes

predator (PRED-uh-tur) an animal that lives by hunting other animals for food

prey (pray) an animal that is hunted by another animal for food

reptile (REP-tile) a cold-blooded animal that crawls across the ground or creeps on short legs; most have backbones and reproduce by laying eggs

INDEX

Page numbers in **bold** indicate images.

ABOUT THE AUTHOR

Jay Leslie has always loved to write. Everywhere she goes, she carries a notebook just in case she gets a new idea. Most of all, she loves to write the books that she wishes she'd had as a child.